My Restaurant Is On Fire

JAHZMIN FRENCH

MY RESTAURANT IS ON FIRE

My Restaurant Is On Fire

Copyright © 2019 Culture Catalyst LLC

All rights reserved.

No Part of this publication may be reproduced, distributed, or transmitted in any form or by any means, including photography, recording, or other electronic or mechanical methods, without prior written permission of the publisher. Except in the case of brief quotations embodied in critical reviews and certain noncommercial uses permitted by copyright law.

Written by Jahzmin French

ISBN :978-1-798-55398-5

DEDICATION

I dedicate this book to Restaurant Owners, Managers, and Executive leaders that are open to learn a new solution to the old problems they may face and that have a desire to conquer their current culture downfalls and loop holes. I also dedicate this book to leaders, who are grooming and developing other managers within their company so that they can be empowered to operate more successfully in their roles. This book was created to encourage managers who are currently reconstructing the culture to keep pushing through no matter what; it will be worth all the friction. I allocate this book to anyone in the industry that has a desire to pursue a leadership position in the future and wants to be able to ensure the right culture for their brand. In addition, I would like to dedicate this book to the restaurant leaders that helped to mold me during my management journey; they held me accountable for every aspect as a leader with no sugar coating. Phillip Robinson, Brian Smith, and Robert Green thank you for the deposits you made in my career. I plan to educate, help, and hold others accountable as you have for me, so they will find success in their restaurant's culture change.

"The growth and development of people is the highest calling of leadership"

-Harvey S. Firestone

CONTENTS

Recognition

Introduction

1. The G.O.A.T — 6
2. Lights, Camera, Attrition — 13
3. Anybody but a Dead Body — 23
4. The Morale Thief — 31
5. Someone Call 9-1-1 — 38
6. Eighty Six — 47
7. The X Factor — 57
8. Change is Good, Not — 67
9. 38 Hot — 75
10. Burnout Battleground — 84

MY RESTAURANT IS ON FIRE

"May the God of hope fill you with all joy and peace

as you trust him, so that you may overflow with hope by the power

of the Holy Spirit."

Romans 15:13

RECOGNITION

First, I would like to give all the glory to my Heavenly Father, because without God I wouldn't be here today and have the opportunity to show support and love to His people. A genuine thank you to my parents Thomas and Darlene who have always supported me trough numerous trials and tribulations, showing endless love and respect. They have truly transformed from parental leaders into my best friends. I would like to acknowledge Daniel and Arelia for being such a blessing to me and for relentlessly sharing their resources with me and my children. Thank you for the moments you both created to educate and encourage me to seek a fulfilled future in God. I would also like to recognize Steve and Erin for their transparency and unfiltered, sincere advice on ways to achieve my dreams and for holding me accountable to putting action to it. I truly appreciate my brother Darreyel who states his continuous admiration for me as a woman and a mother. I possess a sterling delight in watching him live, work, and grow. He is one of the best educators in the field hands down and I look up to him, for his dedication. I would like to recognize my good friend Anthino, a loving father and husband who has tackled restaurant operations with me in the past and truly shares the passion for food safety, quality, and presentation as I do. I would like to also recognize one of my best friends, Taujuanna, who always gives me courage, new ideas and never lets me forget my true worth by reminding me what I bring to the table. I have never met someone so determined, loyal, and driven in my entire life and for that I admire her greatly.

      There have been many people that have deposited things into my life whether it was advice, education, morale support, money, encouragement, or a simple, loving hug when I needed it. I'm truly grateful for the blessings I have had the opportunity to receive, but thrilled to see the blessings God has reserved for me and my family. My goal is take these deposits people have made in my life, cash out, and place my investments in helping and coaching others in many ways all over the world while enhancing their view on success and life.

INTRODUCTION

There are over one million restaurants in the United States, and collectively, they generate over $800 billion in sales making up over ten percent of the nation's workforce. Reports show that 90% of restaurant managers, along with 80% of restaurant owners, began at entry level which is a drastic shift in operating roles. One of the many responsibilities of a manager is to uphold company values and display actions that reflect a business's mission statement, and this is extremely vital when it comes to holding staff accountable for the same results. Your business can have some of the best practices in place to pave the way for smooth operations and increased profits, but if there is no leadership dedicated to accountability those systems will fall by the way side and die, killing the business along with it. This is why I focus so much on the delegation, execution and development with managers because the life of a business is primarily in your hands. Individually speaking, the restaurant industry is a limitless highway for career growth; that does not require a squeaky clean background, a long overly detailed resume, but rather looks at an applicant's values, talent and willingness to learn and execute while on the job. I encourage people everywhere I go to give the restaurant industry a try because it will change your life and could present so many new opportunities.

With over fifteen years of experience in the restaurant industry, I have worked progressively in many positions, always wanting more. I have made many mistakes, received violations on inspections and I have even mismanaged some situations on my journey and now I have a desire to give other managers and owners the shortcut so they will not suffer as I did. In this book I share many personal stories from multiple perspectives which include being a server, key holder, bartender, assistant manager, certified trainer, assistant general manager and general manager. I also address the types of unwanted challenges and events that can bring destruction to a business's culture explaining how to handle them and how leaders can prevent them all together. I have also included an interactive journal at the end of each section so that you can work with your team, layout your challenges, self examine, and be the catalyst toward enhancing the culture and creating a better work environment. It's a proven fact that happier employees deliver a better guest experience and decreases turnover, which will in return grow sales and ultimately increase profit. There are also verses of reference that readers can use to further study and correlate what the Bible says about certain topic in each section throughout this book. Leaders, remember your challenges are not exclusive and you are not alone, it's time to transform your mindset and get to work with your team and I hope this book inspires, encourages, and pushes you along the way to operational success.

SECTION ONE

"The G.O.A.T"

"A leader is one who knows the way, goes the way, and shows the way."

-John C. Maxwell

The restaurant bug bit me very early in life as a 17 year old high school girl, when I landed my first job with a 24 hour restaurant known for their steak burgers and milkshakes. I took so much pride in putting on my apron, bow tie, and clipping my swipe card to my hip before getting dropped off to work. I was a total restaurant geek and I didn't even realize it at the time, but I unconsciously signed a lifelong deal with the restaurant industry and I would never be able to disconnect. While in college I usually kept between two and three jobs and after working in a few good bars and full service restaurants I wanted to do just a little more beyond waiting tables. I got the opportunity to become a certified trainer and then some time later I was presented with the opportunity to lead shifts as a key holder. I loved my new roles and I still had the chance to continue waiting tables as well so in my book I was truly winning. Years down the road I was asked to consider restaurant management and I verbally declined without much hesitation, I never really witnessed a really happy manager before, so I was sure that role was not for me, but obviously it didn't stop there. After a long night of my mind replaying the voice asking me about the promotion I submitted my updated resume and after a couple of interviews and a background check I was promoted. In all of my 15 years of restaurant experience, being a restaurant manager was the hardest thing I have ever done in my entire life. I truly feel that going into labor with both my children and naturally evacuating them from body was easier than managing a restaurant. Maybe it's because the labor pains go away perhaps. When calculating the growing pains of me as a new manager along with the challenges of the operation there was a slight fear that I wasn't the right nurturer for the business. When managing a restaurant you can be figuratively "pregnant" or expectant, with the hopes of hiring all the right staff with each interview, increasing your sales always beating the previous year, having the cleanest facility in the land, and successfully banking on the company's bonus program. So let's just call those weeks on our sales calendars "trimesters" which is a period of three months and managers should be encouraged to create 30,60, and90 day plans for pursuing profit and success, so the term trimester seems fitting. Naturally with each trimester your mindset is changing you notice all the business coaches and restaurant gurus possibly didn't prepare you for EVERYTHING. You begin to emotionally and physically feel the changes of your restaurant and you can see your business, which is your baby is growing and developing really quickly. During this development you prepare for the birth of creative ideas, sales driven strategies and being able to become a better leader. When it's time to give birth you go through the first stage which is the onset of true labor and when searched the first definition given for labor is "work, especially hard physical work" and this is what it takes in some areas of your restaurant while majority of the areas will require your cognitive side to perform. You have to sometimes get more involved and work beside your team and possibly break a sweat getting through high volumes while somehow still leading the way and this is a challenging balance to accomplish. Leaders need to learn the operation by doing the work themselves because the more hands on experience you have knee deep in the business the better you will perform in problem solving when something goes completely haywire, confirming that a little labor helps in a big way.

    During my initial three months at the first restaurant I ever managed which was a very popular restaurant chain known for its world famous wings in Pensacola, Florida a fryer caught fire, the roof leaked in almost every section, my general manager asked me to terminate a cook without out his supervision, a keg line busted, the a/c went out, the hood vents went out, a guest drove their car into a water pipe and cut off our supply, walk in cooler stopped working, a soda bag got sliced, paychecks were accidently sent out of state and so much more. Although this was quite a bit, I can honestly say I appreciated every struggle because it truly prepared me mentally and I was able to train myself on utilizing my time to find a solution and not waste it by dancing the "panic shuffle" for twenty minutes. Even the moments when employees decided to not show up, I reminded myself "don't waste time freaking out". Often, I had to step up my game plan and work in their place and I learned not be frustrated but used it as a chance to see how long it took to get things done so that way I could manage a cook, hopefully a new more reliable cook, about time management when performing certain tasks so they weren't convinced they had the opportunity to daily milk the clock which saved on labor dollars and helped to increased productivity.

Managers that have the ability to jump in and work alongside their cooks or servers, being the support they need in a rush while displaying a great attitude, are absolutely golden. Your team, big or small, will respect and appreciate the modern minded manager that is not just barking orders and pointing fingers but is a true leader that doesn't mind a little dirt under their nails and a spot of grease on their slacks. This is the foundation for a great manager that will keep staff in your restaurant because the leadership is one they can go to for support and actually receive it.

1Timothy 3:2

"Now the overseer is to be above reproach, faithful to his wife temperate, self-controlled, respectable. Hospitable, able to teach."

If you are willing to become this type of manager and can stand tall through all the labor pains of your business, you should have a team that respects you and is ready to be led by you in no time, so now it's time to truly PUSH! You need to PUSH daily goals by informing your staff of where you are and where you need to be, strategize on how you will reach them. PUSH the goal of always trying to find or develop the next best employee to enhance your guest's experience. PUSH continuous training in your store to empower your employees so they can have successful guest interactions and properly perform in their roles. PUSH a clean culture so food safety remains a priority and health inspections continue to be a success. PUSH alignment within your leadership and communication to better serve your staff and then after all the laboring and pushing,

Congratulations you're the parent of a well managed restaurant! Love, Nurture, be Consistent and always strive to become Greater.

> **"Your work is going to fill a large part of your life and the only way to be truly satisfied is to do what you believe is great work. The only way to do great work is to love what you do"**
>
> -Steve Jobs

What is your biggest operational challenge and what ways could you improve? When will an action plan be complete to reflect the needed adjustments?

_____

_____

_____

_____

What job or position are you most unfamiliar with in your restaurant? Which staff member would you choose to properly and genuinely show you the ropes?

_____

_____

_____

_____

Would your team say you're the manager they can go to every time for support and actually receive it? Why or why not? And if not in what way could you shake that stigma?

_____
_____

_____
_____

In what ways will you lead the charge to improve your management team's alignment so that when pushing goals, practicing food safety and on the job training you can truly benefit the restaurants culture?

_____
_____

_____
_____

SECTION TWO

"Lights, Camera, Attrition"

> **"In order to build a rewarding employee experience, you need to understand what matters to your people"**
>
> **-Julie Bevacqua**

As I watched the DreamWorks Pictures film Dreamgirls and indulged in the scene where Jennifer Hudson slowly sings "What about what I need, what about what's best for me, What about how I feel, What about me" I truly connected because, I was the server picking up the tables no one wanted, running all the food since every server went completely deaf when their name was called in the pickup window and personally I appreciated the value of hot food going out instead of handing that guest their cheeseburger with an odd yellow latex appearance from sitting under the heat lamp too long. I was the server that stayed late, came early, and picked up shifts for the girl that call out with a repeat hangover every weekend; the reason she was ever scheduled past Thursday was beyond me. Don't even ask about employees participating in shift running side work. I think the rest of the staff thought the instructions were to continue "running away" from the side work. Just typing this is sending me into a frustrated flashback, but nevertheless, I hung in there. I actually wanted to be the type of employee that my managers could count on, but over time where was the benefit? I was internally singing Jennifer Hudson's theatrical lyrics and rethinking my loyalty.

Managers, with poor culture being one of the top ten reasons why employees quit their jobs and lack of appreciation being in the top 5 reasons, you have to improve these areas of your restaurant immediately. Personally speaking, they both go hand in hand and when focused on together you can get a tremendous result. You must create an environment of clear communication and ensure tasks are evenly distributed on appropriate levels. Be sure to schedule a one on one meeting with each employee, to coach your team through weaknesses and encourage progression and teamwork in every position of your restaurant. This should be done at least every quarter. It is said that "teamwork divides the tasks and multiplies the success" and it's your responsibility to make this happen. Yes, I understand that you have a business to run and setting aside individual coaching time can seem in far reach but if you have an aligned management team you can evenly divide and conquer. For example if you have a three person management team and thirty employees each manager evaluates just ten employees to keep them on track, developing them in to what type of worker your business needs while keeping them on your payroll. Employees actually like the feedback and they feel better doing their jobs and it encourages them to stay employed longer. According to a recent survey 46% of restaurant managers and owners said that hiring is their number one challenge. Despite the validity of this unfavorable task don't keep the servers that don't take tables or run food employed in your business. There is absolutely no room for them in the budget, they will cause you to lose sales and will possibly send your all star server, that discreetly carries the extra loads, to the bistro across the street where management has created structure and recognizes hard work. There will be nothing you can do about it. And this, my friends, is a taste of attrition.

Proverbs 27:23-24

"Be sure you know the condition of your flocks, give careful attention to your herds, for riches do not endure forever, and a crown is not secure for all generations"

Reduction of high turnover, or attrition, can happen with a changed mindset and only a few committed steps. First you need to enhance your training, if you don't have a training program in place; you need to have one designed immediately. Even the disciples had to be trained by Jesus in order to properly do their jobs, why wouldn't you train your staff to properly operate in your business? You may need new employees pretty quickly sometimes but, there is no point in hiring a few new staff members just so you can lead them down an unorganized or uninformative path with no tools to get the work properly done in your restaurant. This will only aggravate both parties during operation so having a clear, useful, and efficient program will be a way to help eliminate this particular headache all together. With a quality training program, employees will feel empowered and ready to perform in their hired roles. Too many times in restaurants the first day of training is "can you make me two cokes and a water and take it to table 13?" when the new guy doesn't even know where the bathroom is located let alone a table number since no one thought to even give him a tour of the building he was hired to work in. This cannot happen. Secondly, hire the right people. Bill Gates once said "I choose a lazy person to do a hard job, because a lazy person will find an easy way to do it" and kudos to him for finding success with that type of employee but of course this is a no-go for restaurant operators in their selection process. Lazy is not allowed. Be sure to consider an applicant's personality, communication ability, team player attitude and overall skill set. Applicants know what's expected of them at the very beginning, this is our chance as managers to set the bar of our business's expectations.

    Years ago I was looking for a place to live and the owner of one property I found had only two demands to pay rent and maintain the property he didn't have time for confetti, or unnecessary things. When it came to hiring Back of the House employees and years of using the corporate template of suggested questions with no true way to filter out the bad apples before it was too late, I learned to just cut right to the chase. I told them they must be reliable, take care of the food, work clean, follow spec at all times, and respect their leadership as well as coworkers. At any time they were unable to do these things I made it clear, I didn't need them. In your restaurant pick the things that are non-negotiable and of high priority for every shift and focus on those topics to form your interview questions. The best time to make these demands is during the interview and readdressed in orientation because let's be honest, any person looking for a job is a "yes man" when they initially get on board. If you are one of the few restaurants that do not hold an orientation with new employees, start now. Orientation should be informative, giving a blueprint to what their job lintels along with basic rules. Now you will be able to hold employees accountable with the foundation you both agreed to, because like the old saying goes "things don't end wrong, they start wrong" so be sure to get your new hires off on the right foot.

Lastly, managers you must enhance recognition in your restaurant. Do simple gift cards or even throw a donut, taco, or pizza party in honor of the staff member or members you would like to recognize. Be smart and creative while keeping the budget in mind, you can keep it simple or make a big, showboat presentation, in the end the logistics doesn't matter but it will go a very long way in the hearts of your staff. I truly love scrolling through my Linkedin feed seeing the businesses that have mastered employee recognition and it just makes me wish I worked for those companies, so I know the employees can't have a huge desire to jump ship. Give your employees feedback on performance and consider opportunities for promotion. Most employees stick with companies where growth is possible and this minimizes the revolving door of shotgun new hires for you as well. We have all had that regular guest sitting at a table that looks around and says "I see a lot of new faces" and they notice because they learn to build those relationships as well. Be sure you try retaining your valuable staff with these given steps in conjunction with any future new hires so everyone is jumping from the same platform, because in the restaurant industry guests come for the experience and they like seeing familiar staff so let's make sure we give them what they came for. You have to be the captain of the ship and the anchor hen the sails are torn owning these responsibilities. Also you must know what direction you want to see your business go in and give confirmation that you are going to lead the charge, guiding your team to that destination step by step.

"The best way to predict the future is to create it"

- Abraham Lincoln

What is the first area in your restaurant's culture that has the greatest challenge? What are two ways you can enhance those areas and do you have a team of people to ignite the change?

_____
_____

_____
_____

Which leader on your management team is least effective at communicating in your business? Which is the best at it? Why?

_____
_____

_____
_____

Does your team have assigned Areas of Responsibilities (AOR)? If so, do you have the right people doing the right areas? Is it time to switch it up? If not assigned at all please briefly delegate these to each manager in the lines below.

_____
_____

_____
_____

Do you have staff in your restaurant that cause friction in doing their job or voice that they just simply don't want to do certain job functions that are mandatory to their role? List them. Can this employee be developed? Do they need to be placed in a different position? Is it time to replace them? Put together an action plan for this employee and give them a time frame to comply.

_____
_____

_____
_____

Do you have a proper training program in place? Does it need to be modified or updated? Is there an employee handbook or code of conduct administered to each new hire? If not how will you obtain these for your business?

_____
_____

_____
_____

Is there room for growth, pay increase, and promotion? Is there a position you can create that employees can set as a reachable goal so they can thrive? What is that position and what are the requirements?

_____
_____

_____
_____

_____
_____

How do you recognize your employees when they reach a goal or just simply have a good shift or good week in sales? What ideas can you deliver on in this area? Don't forget to pat yourself on the back when you obtain small victories.

_____

_____

_____

_____

SECTION THREE

"Anybody but a Dead Body"

"Strength and growth come only through continuous effort and struggle"

-Napoleon Hill

As a newer assistant general manager at a seasonal location, during summer, I was attempting to post my schedules and a really huge problem began to stick out and I needed to come up with a quick solution or I was screwed. The business would be screwed! As I stared this problem in the face I could feel the anxiety creeping its way into my chest like a room filling up with smoke just before the flames arrive to burn anything it could attach itself to. If anyone reading this book has ever experienced restaurant level anxiety they will appreciate my dramatic description, it sucks." So what could be that bad?" you are probably wondering. Little do you realize it's a problem you more than likely have also had to face while running a restaurant. As I was getting toward the weekend for that particular schedule I was writing, a complication began to form, there were just not enough employees to schedule to effectively operate. We were projected to be short handed from time we opened the doors until the last entrée was walked from the expo window at the end of each weekend night. What now? I needed to hire. By hire I mean put on the schedule. By put on the schedule I mean within the next 24 hours leaving time to train. This was going to be a hot restaurant mess. Although in the last chapter I discussed the true benefits of hiring the right person and I truly mean it, I have to be 100 percent honest with myself, so that I can transparently help others. Let's face it folks I was a real life restaurant operator so I must discuss one of the ugly sides of staffing in this industry so I can successfully coach you through it while remaining true to the game.

John 15:16

"You did not choose me, but I chose you and appointed you so that you should go and bear fruit and that your fruit should abide, so that whatever you ask the father in my name, he may give it to you."

As a manager you may get to the point when you have to choose a "body" even if all that body can do is wash dishes, keep the floor swept and run trash, at first, you will take what you can get. Do not feel convicted for this decision, but I want to tell you how to turn the unqualified into the ultrasonic for your business. In the restaurant industry there is an extreme shortage of talent to hire and for some operators, depending on their location, it can seem like finding the needle in the heaping food and beverage haystack and it really puts a squeeze on owners and general managers when it comes down to staffing and scheduling for operation. Managers, in order to ease some of the stress from this dilemma and take back control you must first change your mindset and open yourself up to knowing that sometimes you should not to hire for talent but hire for potential. Take a minute to consider what could be the transformation experienced as a result of your enhanced restaurant training when hiring the unqualified. I took a certain joy in hiring an employee with very little to no experience because they were like putty in my hand. I was able to mold them into exactly what I wanted them to be. They didn't have the long resume advertising an unsteady bounce from business to business picking up bad habits along the way while developing a "little miss know it all" or "big man on campus" mentality. Another benefit of hiring someone with less experience will be lower pay rate expectations and comfortable room for performance based increases, good for labor cost as well as your bottom line and you really win when the employee is developed into your "go-to" girl or guy, becoming an asset to your restaurant. This type of employee usually develops a true sense of pride in their job having worked their way up from the bottom, being handed scarce responsibilities to now possibly running shifts throughout the week, they will be one to keep around. If you can accomplish recruiting hires like these, this type of developmental success will embed loyalty and those employees will be a walking billboard of future employment and good referrals for the business. This will help you jump and clear the turnover hurdle.

    One night I went out to a restaurant with a friend and our server was so polite, her menu knowledge was perfect, she was confident and very prompt. I knew within the first few minutes of my visit that I was going to recruit her to come and work for me, I couldn't help myself. When I asked her how she liked working there and if she felt as though she made good money she smiled with wonder of my random questions not sure what to say. Long story short I was successful and in no time she was in orientation and off to start training. I learned the few challenges she had very quickly and gave her advice and coached her to the perfect employee. She later brought her friend to work for me who was phenomenal and second friend who was great and lastly, her twin sister who was a joy to work with. This is one of the best examples of successful recruiting in my entire career and although I have moved up and moved on she still enjoys working for that company and thrives daily.

As a manager, it's your responsibility to get to know your staff, learn what their strengths and weaknesses are then develop them in the proper areas to so they can be empowered. If you don't understand each of your employees' strengths you haven't spent enough time connecting with them and you should do this as soon as possible letting them know what your restaurant has to offer them. Give your staff new opportunities to grow. For example you may have a dish guy that has the ability to post all your social media daily and he can acquire the title of "Franchise Marketing Lead" which will prompt him to actually have a desire to do more and give him a sense of entitlement other than being known as the guy that clears the overwhelming dish pit each shift. In the process of changing your mindset about hiring just anybody to fill that spot on your schedule and actually developing your "instant staff" you will soon make important discoveries about yourself in the process, because you play a direct role in the process of your restaurants success. You will feel an exclusive joy when looking at your team that you had to mold and build, seeing how far you all have come, and it is priceless.

> "Great things in business are never done by one person"
>
> - Steve Jobs

When it comes to scheduling for operations, are schedules posted in a timely fashion so that your employees can plan for the week? If not, what will be your new "due or die" day to post?

_____
_____

_____
_____

In your restaurant would it benefit managers to write the schedule starting with the event days and weekend first and then work your way backwards to Monday? This may help with proper distribution of hours for the busier shifts in your restaurant. What manager would have the toughest time with this adjustment if implemented? Why?

_____
_____

_____
_____

Do you experience no show interviewees? Have you surveyed the local area to take in account what surrounding businesses are paying in salary for new staff? If not when will you get this done? If you have what plan will you put in place to keep up?

_____
_____

_____
_____

Are you confident with the idea of hiring for potential over talent level? What are your reservations? What two ways can your conquer those fears?

_____
_____

_____
_____

Are your management and training teams aligned and ready to put in the extra coaching needed to pull new hires through the ranks while inspiring them along the way? Which manager or trainer will take the longest to get on board? Should they be a part of this process?

_____
_____

_____
_____

SECTION FOUR

"The Morale Thief"

"Tell the negative committee that meets inside your head to sit down and shut up"

-Ann Bradford

"Hey girl, I like the way you bend over when you put that bus tub back!" is what I heard yelled from the kitchen window after running dishes to the back of house and returning the bus tub to the wait station. After turning my head and identifying the source of this disrespectful comment, I quickly walked off the dining room floor forced; the side kitchen saloon doors open, stepped up to the arrogant cook whose daily attitude was like poison and let him know that I would not tolerate that type of interaction. I absolutely hated working with him, but he was one of the few cooks always got the food out on time and it looked great. I guess this is why he was employed so long? As time went on he did not stop with his inappropriate comments and also disrespected management from time to time, he was the definition of a workplace bully. The type of environment he was turning my workspace into; encouraged me to consider looking for another venue to earn income in peace. Why do they let him act this way? I always wondered. "Aren't there rules against this type of behavior? A law even?" I always thought to myself.

Managers, you may have a top performing cook or server that can be a bit of a prick to surrounding co workers and they are making the work environment a toxic one. I'm just going to bring to your attention that the morale in a workplace causes more turnover than we may realize. Don't let one little employee, damage, steal or bring down the overall morale in your business. Operators themselves can also be a culprit to lowered workplace morale. Yes I said it! One of the quickest ways this can happen is when a manager doesn't listen to their employees or tends to avoid and or mishandle tough issues that staff may bring to their attention. Also having a bad attitude and seeming aggravated at the mere fact they will actually have to do any work at all repels dependability, quickly killing good morale. During some of my years as an assistant manager, I had a coworker who my staff knew in their heart and soul they couldn't truly depend on to listen and effectively react for the smooth operation of the business. He was neither a good leader nor team player and this truly diminished the thought of being able to lean on him to perform as a superior. They would come to me instead feeling guilty but assertive, knowing they were stopping me from doing ten things and he wasn't attempting even one, but I always responded more than willing to help, but this should not be the culture. Most of the time if he was the only manager on duty our staff would just fend for themselves the best they could until a dire situation occurred and even then he displayed no professionalism and sometimes did not respect employees or guests as deserved. Just think of how damaging this is to the morale of the business. It's happening quite a bit, and possibly in your own restaurant at this very moment. According to recent research high morale has been shown to be a powerful driver of performance. Even more extensive research demonstrates its benefits in productivity, profitability, and customer satisfaction. Low morale may lead to reduced concentration, which in turn can cause mistakes, poor customer service, also contributing to high turnover rates and absenteeism.

Matthew 7:12

"So in everything, do to others what you would have them do to you, for these sums up the Law and the Prophets."

    There are a few ways to increase and maintain employee morale while operating your restaurant. As discussed in a previous chapter, managers should have a one on one session with their staff giving feedback and encouragement but to also listening to them, engaging with questions to fully understand their perspectives and let them know that their work matters. Help your staff to feel valued and be sure to attach an action to what you are hearing from them as well if it will ignite a positive change in your culture. Another way to increase morale that was also previously discussed was employee recognition, which is just a major perk in the working world today and to be successful you must fall in line, and you should honestly feel good doing it. Employee recognition goes a long way and should be performance based so that all deserving parties reap the benefits. Investing in your employees by grooming them on site or even sending them to a hospitality or leadership seminar to kick start growth is always good and it gives them the sense that you believe in them; for that they will have a new respect for your brand. Leaders, get to know your employees. Do they have families? Are they students? What are they majoring in? Do they want to grow in the company or is this just a stepping stone? Do they enjoy working for you? We focus on guest relationships which are top priority but we must realize that as owners and managers we must continue to ignite and build employee relationships as well because it will reflect during customer interactions. It is your job, as the manager, to find this relationship balance along with not allowing the bad apples to stick around or multiply, because when employees are satisfied with their jobs they are motivated to work harder and true loyalty is instilled. So don't let a morale thief come and rob your restaurant employees blind even if the thief is you.

> **"Accountability separates the wishers in life from the action takers that care enough about their future to account for their daily actions."**
>
> **- John Di Lemme**

Do you have a really good employee that you consider to be great for labor or talent, but poisonous? List their names and how long you have employed them. How much longer do you plan to let other employees suffer?

_____

_____

_____

_____

Have you already had employee complaints on a coworker? What was the complaint (big or small)? What way did you resolve it, and did it work? If you have not resolved it already, please write a short plan below on how you will begin to handle this before it gets the chance to fester.

_____

_____

_____

_____

_____

_____

Typically how soon do you and your leaders resolve issues or put in to action resolutions to your legit employee suggestions? Which manager on your team should make this a focus?

_____

_____

_____

_____

_____

_____

_____

Do you have a manager on your team that can use some development when it comes to respecting the hourly staff? Name them. List examples of ways they have become the morale thief. List the first thing they must resolve about this challenge immediately.

_____

_____

_____

_____

As an owner or manager have you taken the time to get to know your staff beyond them being just another expense on your P&L? In what ways have you engaged them? If you haven't done this or don't do it often, set an action plan for your leaders to make this happen.

_____
_____

_____
_____

SECTION FIVE

"Someone Call 9-1-1"

"Those who think it is permissible to tell white lies soon grow color-blind"

-Austin O'Malley

One morning while managing, I was looking at the dumpster pad, or outside trash area, to make sure my cooks followed my instruction from the day before. They were to discontinue the spread of trash and debris around the dumpster and leaving it there since it's an unclean habit and will soon begin to attract bugs and rodents. "Looking good" I thought to myself as I approached the entrance but as I walk behind the large container I notice a random blue cooler. I slightly lifted the lid and discovered seven bottles of beer that appear to have come from inside the restaurant's beer cooler floating in thin ice cubes that haven't had the chance to melt yet. I closed it quickly just to reopen it again with hopes of what I was seeing would just disappear and I would not have the displeasure of terminating someone immediately. This really pissed me off. I began to just stare at the floating "hot" (street term for stolen) items thinking of all the good things I did for my staff. Thinking of all the times I truly bent over backwards to make sure they were content working with me as their manager. Thinking of all the times I awarded them food knowing they didn't have money until pay day. Thinking of the times I asked for their input and implemented the changes they desired. Thinking of the times I promoted them to ignite growth, pride, and pay increase. They steal from me? This was not how I saw myself starting my day. I latched my skinny right arm to the handle of the cooler and with frustration I quickly drug it from the dumpster to the back door of the restaurant to place in my office. I drug the cooler so fast out of anger I was expecting a crack or hole to develop from the rough friction of the concrete. Instead I almost tripped over my own two, moving feet. I thought to myself "slow down because falling will only make the day worse". In my office I look inside the cooler once again, with my hands shaking in pure frustration and denial. Now I would have to put on my deerstalker, play detective and get rid of the thief and accomplices.

Proverbs 20:17

"Food gained by fraud tastes sweet, but one ends up with a mouth full of gravel"

Managers you will at some point in your career have an employee steal from you, brace yourself for that. Most of you reading this book already have, possibly on multiple occasions experience this type of moment. There is not some secret formula to completely eliminate theft because people will always find a new way to steal but, there are ways that you can drastically reduce theft in your building. First let's address a few ways the thieves can rob your business while employed. Servers can claim improper tips on credit cards to pocket the extra dough. Not only will these damage consumer relationships but will quickly open the door for civil cases. Another nasty trick servers will use to get a bigger tip will be to tell the managers they know would never follow up and that refuse to touch tables during their guest's experience that there was a problem with the food or drinks after guests leave the table. The bill is paid in full with cash, the lazy manager just swipes to authorize a comp and that extra, unearned twenty bucks goes towards the server getting a pedicure at the spa or a fresh haircut for the weekend. It can feel like taking candy from a baby. But wait there's more. I call this next act the "Soft Drink Shuffle" this is the most common one with servers I have had to manage. This happens when a guest orders a soda, tea or similar product with their meal pays and leaves the building for the day. After that the server can either ask the manager on duty to delete the drink because they ordered it by mistake, product didn't taste right or if they have the ability, they can split it off and use it for the next guest's table. It becomes a profit of about $3.19 or more each time it's moved. If a server in a high volume restaurant can do this for only 15 guests a day that's an extra $47.85 and if they work five shifts a week that's $239.25 in their pocket on top of the honest gratuity during their shifts which is between 18 to 20 percent of their sales. Not a bad salary at all. Those are your sales dollars being stolen and within one year this shuffling act will equal up to over $12,000 and that's if you only have just one server on your roster brave enough to do the shuffle right in front of your eyes, but since thieves are like bloodsucking mosquitoes, if there is one there are more. Here are some ways to fight back and put that money where it rightfully belongs on your P and L. Be sure the Point of Sales security is tailored to request a manager password to do comps, voids, split checks, or table transfers. Also audit checks for drinks being ordered properly, you should also be on the floor getting feedback from patrons you will be able to match the physical orders to the POS orders. Do not transfer drinks have employee ring up the newer drink and you delete the old one, they will then realize that scheme won't work and will eliminate that particular avenue all together. Have a system in place to review credit card tips to what a server's check out or sales report says and if they don't match delete the checkout immediately and make server claim the proper amount. If this happens too often begin holding staff accountable and possibly discuss termination. They are trying to steal.

Proverbs 12:22

"The LORD detests lying lips. But he delights in people who are trustworthy"

In my career I had a Director who taught me much of what I know today. He would tell this story often of some employees stealing at one of his locations as he caught them red handed. It was the best restaurant theft story ever to me knowing he got justice, because this is not always the case. He went into one of the stores in his region and once he left after great deal of time he simply drove the next parking lot and began his own stake out. He knew some cooks were stealing but he wanted to catch them. Sure enough he sees the back door of the restaurant swing open and he watched as one of the cooks brings case after case of food putting it in his trunk each time until he had what he wanted. My director was shocked and angry, but this physical confirmation was worth the wait. His anger grew into passion and that passion led him from his own car to the cook's trunk to retrieve every single case while the cook was inside probably salivating and deciding how he would prepare and season the stolen product before cooking it, something that never belonged to him in the first place. Before getting the cases out of the trunk he called the police and you can guess the ending. Not all businesses get the product back, when its gone it's gone. Don't be the absent and unmentioned manager in this shared story that allowed the culture of stealing to exist to the point of staff being comfortable enough to steal entire cases of food. Some managers have mastered the art of sleeping with their eyes wide open allowing the cost of goods to go through the roof dangling the financial success of the restaurant in the balance.

Owners and managers you must take inventory often so you can track usage, know what you have on hand, and keep an eye on the product or spoilage. You may even create a count sheet where high cost items are counted two to three times daily to pinpoint any loss or theft in a matter of hours. When your staff is aware of a system like this it will discourage them tremendously against taking what isn't their own. Another idea would be to walk to the dumpster with cooks as they deliver trash to outside dumpsters, this is the best opportunity for them to hide stolen product and just simply walk it to their car or stash it away on the property until they return to claim it. It can be very frustrating and even a heavy burden to have to make these provisions to eliminate theft along with all the other responsibilities the operation requires but it must be done. Having an aligned team of managers will broaden this control and awareness work together to reduce and ultimately knockout theft in your business.

> "A society without the means to detect lies and theft soon squanders its liberty and freedom."
>
> -Chris Hedges

Has an employee, which you are aware of, stolen from you? If so how did you handle the situation? If you haven't had this happen to you yet, what steps may you take with that type of employee? Explain why?

_____

_____

_____

_____

Do you have a manager on your team that staff can recognize as the one that will not "follow up" and unknowingly open the door to theft? List them. Put together an action plan for them to take back control.

_____

_____

_____

_____

How often do you and your team do inventory? Does your restaurant inventory on products like liquor, beer, and high cost foods daily? If so are the managers performing this task or hourly staff? If your restaurant is not doing this, explain why. Also add a proposed date to begin.

_____

_____

_____

_____

Do you share your food cost goals along with the current status with your staff? If so, great! Please explain how often and in what form you release this data. Also list other categories in which you would like to begin educating them on as well. If not, explain when and in what ways you will keep staff in the loop of this information, while working towards the desired goals. Please include a consistent deadline on which it will be done.

_____

_____

_____

_____

In what ways will you keep your management team motivated to stay consistent in taking the extra steps to reduce and ultimately eliminate theft and not view it as an extra, unwanted chore?

_____
_____

_____
_____

SECTION SIX

"Eighty-Six"

"Don't be so prepared for the battle, to the point you find yourself unprepared for the victory! When you truly believe in yourself, you prepare for it all."

-Qwana M. Reynolds-Frasier

Goosebumps started to rise on my arms as I walked into one of the most amazing restaurants I've ever visited, the décor was like something off of a magazine cover and the smell of sizzling meat tickled my nose. I'm a tiny girl but I love food and I consider eating as one of my hobbies. As a full time working mother of two with many moving parts in my life I didn't get out as much lately and I was thrilled for this opportunity. We were seated by a sweet, adorable host who welcomed us and relayed the name of our server that would be taking care of us after asking if this was our first visit. As we sat there briefly it was like the walls began to sparkle. Every person in the dining area looked excited to be there both guests and employees alike. Picking up a modern, sleek and bountiful menu I remember thinking playfully to myself that I want a little bit of everything. Soon our waiter approached very clean and well put together wearing a smile to match.

"Good evening folks my name is John and I will be in charge of your dining experience tonight. I see you're already taking a look at the menu but I do want to let you know we are out of a few items." The waiter proceeded to name about four menu entrees and one dessert that were not available despite the fact they were printed on the menu.

Two of those items being my first and second dinner choice at first glance. I was very disappointed. But nevertheless I didn't want that to ruin the moment. I quickly browsed the beer list, taking my mind off my briefly trampled hope, and placed an order for two pints of my favorite Indian Pale Ale and ice waters for myself and my date. As the restaurant chatter made the building hum with good times and cheer, our waiter approached our table returning with water and an expression of defeat. He put his chin to his chest, looked in my eyes and informed me that they were out of the beer I ordered. Really, now should I get frustrated? I know it's not his personal fault but this was more than unfair to me, the guest that never gets out, that just wants a meal and a beer that YOUR menu which allows me to think it will provide for me or any other guest upon request. At that point the chatter began to sound like noise, just plain noise. The sleek, vibrant menu book may as well have been toilet paper with the selections written in crayon for how useful it had been to me at this time. I even think the nice glitter I was admiring faded off the walls. Once again, I wasn't sure when I would get to go out and enjoy myself not being surrounded by kids or work so I changed my drink selection to something I didn't truly want. I ordered an entrée I genuinely did not desire. I didn't order a dessert since my belly was too full from my main course of disappointment and trimmings of disenchantment. Because of who I am the server was tipped the average twenty percent since I know that it was not truly his fault, but I would not be a returning guest for a while, if ever. With nice restaurants being on every other block, I rather give another business a try that may not be out of everything they claim to offer.

    Mangers, think of how this server felt, to start his shift

meeting being informed of all the items, or ingredients that were not in house, available, out of stock, or eighty sixed. Having to mentally and emotionally brace himself for the battles he knew he would have to face with unwarned guests sitting at his tables. This puts staff in a position to constantly say things like "I'm sorry" or " I truly apologize" knowing their remorse is viewed to be empty in the eyes of the guests they have to let down. This also gives a server anxiety of possibly reduced tip percentages since they are unable to deliver your brand's version of a true guest experience. Depending on how many ingredients you may be out of can turn a restaurant's dining room into a dungeon for your staff, they don't want to work somewhere that can't keep proper inventory. Another issue to consider is the business that does not have a shift meeting in which managers would disperse vital information to their staff. In this case, cooks or servers don't find out they have depleted supply until a guest has ordered and has now waited twenty to thirty minutes for food they can't even have. How unfair. This is a total let down to your staff, as a leader, to let your operation suffer due to under ordering, under planning and unaligned communication. Most employees want to be effective in their roles but if they are hindered because they lack the resources needed this can dampen the morale and shrivel motivation. Then they cope by making jokes like "we probably out "or "good luck finding one". Especially in the back of house they probe the accusing questions like "who placed the order this week?" or "why do we keep running out? They know we blow through it" This is defeat to them. Some teams may turn on each other asking things like "who did prep this morning" which can further ignite the day shift versus night shift warfare that already exists in most restaurants. They may become bitter and will eventually decrease respect towards the leadership on some level justifying ways to go rogue against the company's policies or mission.

Romans 15:5

"Now the God of patience and consolations grant you to be like-minded one toward another according to Christ Jesus"

I'm going to explain a few reasons why restaurants may hear the term "86" echoed within their operation, but for those who may not be aware, the term "eighty six", means to completely run out of an item or even an ingredient used to properly make an item on your menu. This is true for food, beverages, paper products and chemicals. There are a few origins of how this term came about; I will share my favorite three.

1.) AT-6 (Allowance Type) was the code used by the Navy for decommissioned parts and over time it got shortened to the phonetic sound "86"

2.) During the great depression most soup kitchens used large pots that held 85 cups of soup and fed 85 people so if you were the 86th person in line they have just run out. You got no soup.

3.) During the prohibition, the proprietor of Chumley's had an arrangement with the local police. "Friendly" cops would call Chumley's and say "86" and the owner would immediately hustle patrons out of the back door to 86 Bedford St. This is the most popular legend, and to me it's the most exciting.

Now, let's focus back on ways we sometimes make a day in operations unexciting when running out of product, so we can put them behind us. Managers are taught to keep low inventory in most cases, because the merchandise or goods on your shelf could have been money in the bank. Also, you have too much product that may not move as fast as its needs to and may spoil, becoming a complete financial loss. Theft can also be reduced when inventories are low. For example, a cook may steal a steak more easily if there are twenty two of them on a rack but may not feel comfortable stealing if there are only four to five knowing the missing product would be more noticeable to management or even coworkers. Some restaurants are seasonal and their volumes do a complete 360 depending on the time of year which makes it more difficult to stock and properly order the right things at the right times with their operational pace going from 0 to 100. Another reason restaurants run out is due to managers doing what we in the industry call "blind ordering" because in the back of our mind we walk our stores enough to know, we touch our products enough to know, and we see our supplies enough to know what to order. This is a delusional mindset and managers need to properly follow through with ordering procedures and get it right.

There was a very young General Manager, for a restaurant in which I was consulting for, and he was truly a hard worker and possessed a passion for the industry. Unfortunately, his roadmap to management for this particular brand was from server directly into a General Manager position. Before you give a big gasp like I wanted to do, please note the reality that there are more restaurant making this same type of decision if not extremely similar. Due to his plate being so full and not having mastered time management, amongst other leadership skills just yet, he would often place the restaurant's orders very quickly and last minute. One day I asked him how he got done placing the truck orders so fast and I expressed that I barely saw him go into the coolers and I must be honest, he completely shocked me with his response. He let me know that he just pulls up the previous order template on the accounts dashboard and just simply hits the "reorder" button to place his previous grocery order to mimic the products for the week to come. I stood there in front of him completely quiet as I let this insane strategy sink in and process in my mind. So to give a quick back story I noticed during my assessments that the restaurant was out of little things like condiments and paper products along with some food items and the staff had no problem confirming their frustrations stating that this was normal and happens all the time. This is what placing blind orders in your restaurant will result in. Not only will you run out of product, but you will not able to track usage and determine if you should order more or less of an item according to your business. As my pastor once said, this is what I call a manager who has "mastered the art of sleeping with their eyes wide open".

1 Thessalonians 5:6

"So then let us not sleep as others do, but let us be alert and sober"

Here's the good news, there are ways to master the ordering process to insure that your business has the products it needs to operate and make revenue. Managers must track food, beer, and liquor orders which will give you crystal clear insight to your location's usage, spoilage, or waste. Know you restaurant's volume by looking historically at your projected sales and continuously keeping records for years to come. If you have good point of sale programs you can even break your sales down by the hour on specific days in the previous year and beyond. This can save you a ton of money in labor dollars because you will be able to consciously stagger in staff at the projected, high volume times. By knowing the projected volume you can make a sound decisions on purchasing goods and not always falling for the bulk buy and buy only what the business needs, no more no less. When you track your orders you can compare side by side and easily notice discrepancies that appear odd and may be a sure sign of theft or intentional waste. Speaking of waste, there should be a waste sheet readily available that managers have to sign once a product is unsellable and should be a tool to hold staff accountable as well. Have a prep list that will include proper pars and task time frames so productivity is streamlined. All prep sheets should be filled out by managers or authorized shift leaders only. Managers, don't forget to adjust your store's par levels for the projected business, you don't want staff to over prep or be underprepared on the next shift and run out. The leadership on this vital part of operating your business must be properly aligned and execution needs to be precise and if any hourly employees cause friction on following thorough with instructions remind them that "86" isn't just for food it's for people too!

***Side Note: Please make it clear to your staff they do not have the authority to throw away any products without permission. You may be owed a credit from your distributor and managers must be involved in order to accurately receive it.

"You can have all the right strategy in the world if you don't have the right culture, you're dead.

- Patrick Whitesell

Do you hold shift meetings to inform staff of out of stock items or even of items they need to push to get out of inventory? How long are these meetings? Do they work? If not, what needs to be done differently?

_____
_____

_____
_____

How do you track your food, liquor and beer orders? If you are not, when will you start? Do you record your "on hand" and order amount to track usage? Is it helpful?

_____
_____

_____
_____

Have you created a prep sheet and waste log for your daily operations? If not, when will it be available? Who fills out the prep sheets in your restaurant? Do managers have to sign off on waste log? Which leader on your team has challenges with keeping these tools updated?

_____
_____

_____
_____

SECTION SEVEN

"THE X FACTOR"

"To expect the unexpected shows a thoroughly modern intellect"

-Oscar Wilde

The British reality television music competition created by Simon Cowell, although very entertaining, is not the direction we are going with this section. Yet, I'm going to discuss ways to brace yourself when expecting the unexpected in your business, a little something I call the "X Factor". The letter 'X' is often used in algebra to mean "a value that is not yet known" and our responsibility in most businesses, is to "know" since that's how we are able to make the best decisions for our operation. Owners and managers there are going to be some things in your business that you will just simply not see coming your way and this is something many, if not all, operators face from time to time. I'm referring to the events that happen in your business that are not routine, normal, or known to happen. As an owner or manager having all your ducks in a row for a day in operations such as proper line checks, staffing, completed orders, clean facility etcetera, we must still prepare to expect the unexpected, but why? Of course we have all heard of Murphy's Law "anything that can go wrong will go wrong" and it's just that simple and easy to be in a pickle even after you have dotted every I and crossed every T during your day to day.

***Side Note: Loss of water, loss of electricity, supply shortages, construction, food borne illnesses, accidents, computer system failure, data theft, robbery, and violent protests are all possible examples of "the x factor" directly proving Murphy's Law in your business.

> *"Problem Solving is a Restaurant Manager's Superpower."* —Jahzmin French

Managers this is where you have to truly launch your ability to problem solve so that you can reduce negative impacts on your overall business. Along with prioritizing your emergencies you have to be able to take charge, delegate and get your hands dirty to extinguish the "operational fires" that ignite out of the blue. I'm talking about those events that no one typed up as an inclusive part of your manager training manual that you were handed in the beginning of your career. Talk about a missing piece to the puzzle, right? The events in your career that you can credit to "learning as you go" are the type of situations that will be a true challenge that no one may have prepared you for in any way. Even though you may be working hard at fixing an unexpected event, you must keep in mind that the business cannot miss a beat. Your restaurant still has entrees to prepare, delivery orders to be processed or checked, and guests in your seats that deserve a great experience and you must not let them smell, see or sense the smoke coming from the theoretical fire you and your team are working on putting out.

Neither my hands nor my toes can help me count the number of x factors I have had occur in my career, but as stated in the beginning of this book, I have a true appreciation for every single one of them. One morning while managing a restaurant in Jupiter, Florida I was finishing up my opening paperwork and a cook peeked into my office and asked me who the opening server was for the day, after I answered and he commented on them being late, I peeked at the time in the bottom right corner of my laptop, slightly puzzled and I quickly agreed with him and searched for her phone number. Minutes later he returned asking who the opening bartender was supposed to be, indicating neither one was inside the building setting up the restaurant as usual, now I was concerned and began searching my brain with how it could be that I had no front of the house staff getting ready for our guests. Were the openers not scheduled at the proper time and how could I have missed that? I went to investigate but found that everyone was scheduled as needed so I called the bartender who explained to me she was way too sick to work and spent all night reaching out to get her shift covered but no one would come in for her. She also took it upon herself and made the decision not to call the restaurant's phone to inform me, the manager on duty of this vital news. It's a bartender for goodness sake that's not a simple position to always fill on the fly. The missing server, once contacted, explained she overslept and missed the city bus and would be extremely late, so now I had to set up the bar and the dining room for lunch while calling around to see who I could convince to work the bar shift I needed covered, not to mention, we were opening for business in just twenty minutes. As I began power walking, at times running, getting lights on, televisions on, rugs out in the proper places, and heating the tea urns to begin the brewing process, my cook emerges from the back and announces to me that the flattop grill was lit and working but seems to have gone out and he couldn't get the pilot to relight. Trust me we were going to need that grill with fresh, grilled chicken salads and great burgers flying out of our kitchen every lunch shift as if they were free. I laughed. I would always laugh to myself when I was handed unbelievable tasks or information that deliberately works against what I'm trying to do. Why was this happening to me? I thought to myself. As anxiety began to rise during my race against time I kept thinking to prioritize, execute, and move on while keeping a smile. It was only the beginning of the day and I had a long way to go so there was no reward in me letting these crazy circumstances tangle up my emotions.

      Although, there was one event in my career when my emotional strength was very faint on a day that I will never forget while managing in a high volume restaurant on Pensacola Beach known for their great wings and unique staff. It was truck day, the coolers were organized, rotated cleaned and ready for our incoming delivery. Our team always did a pretty good job at having our storage ready to go because in the summer months the demand for groceries was high due to our increased sales volume and we really had to safely pack it in. Noticing the time and realizing our order was late the food distributor was contacted for an E.T.A in which we were quoted time was not accurate. Our delivery showed up about 5 hours late! In the midst of the waiting game we are open, we are busy, and we are sending wings out of our kitchen left and right as usual. Over the hum of the working hoods and sound of the fryers a cook yells "there are only two cases of wings left" my heart dropped into my stomach as I quickly locked eyes with the other manager and, reflecting fear. After calling the sales representative for another ETA on our delivery we were quoted another hour. This was unbelievable. We called our area supervisor and he instructs us not to run out, but get to an approved store and get the food we needed. My coworker goes to the store and returns just in time as we were pulling the very last wings in the house out of the fryer to be shaken and plated. "Thank God, perfect timing" I said to him with a relieved smile on my face. Two of my cooks quickly grab the bags from his hands and start unpacking the meat, as I looked down I couldn't believe what my eyes were seeing. He purchased whole chicken legs and thighs for us to cook, like the meat you find in a Church's© or Popeye's© and when confronted he said "it said drumstick on the package and the purchase of the thighs was a mistake". I think my breath completely left my body in this moment. This was not one of the laughing moments deflecting anger I mentioned before; I was in a living nightmare. What was I supposed to tell our full house of guests that were already waiting for the wings they ordered that were supposedly being prepared? My cooks were looking to me for direction and I was dumbfounded and frozen from the absolute shock of the situation we had all been put in. I finally yell "just cook the chicken these people have to eat and we need to give them something". The drumsticks took much longer than our original large wings to cook, way longer, this felt like a slow ride to Misery Mountain and I wanted to jump out of the window. Once we got the first batch out we made the decision to serve one leg per two wing count so if a guest ordered ten wings they got five drumsticks instead. These plates quickly came back to the kitchen with refusal from almost every guests, no one wanted them. I even had a guest come to our food window and curse me out for the wait and horrible product and I honestly let him, absorbing the verbal punches, because they had every right in my mind to do so. In the midst of my verbal beating and shocking disappointment, a cook said "I think the truck is in the parking lot" I grabbed four cooks and as we confirmed, we headed toward the truck. The driver had a hard time parking and wanted to adjust his trailer, I told him to stay where he was and allow us to grab wings to cook right away. Blocking traffic, we made an assembly line hauling cold cases of fresh chicken wings from the truck's side door, down the ramp, up the staircase, and directly to the kitchen to begin frying, we felt almost normal again. The driver of the truck mentioned traffic and going to his other stops first as his tardy pass, but I was too focused and angry to do anything more than check in the order and sign, I had a restaurant to stabilize.

Proverbs 3:5-7

"Trust in the Lord with all your heart. Never rely on what you what you think you know.

Remember the Lord in everything you do, and he will show you the right way."

    The events you encounter on an unusual day could have you scratching your head in confusion and amazement but problems are just simply a part of the business. Your job as the leader is to figure out the simple key that satisfies all involved parties and then successfully execute them. In the event a problem strikes in your restaurant you must first stay positive, your staff will feed off your energy and follow suite so they need to know that you are confident enough to get through anything your operation can throw at you. If you become negative they will follow and possibly develop a grey area of whether or not you may be the right person the steer the ship and the respect they have for you may begin to dissolve. Transparency is another important trait to display when things go awry; you should let your staff feel that you trust them enough to disclose all information so they have a well rounded understanding of what may be taking place. This will also allow them to share ideas or valid questions that can indirectly prompt you to create a better solution than the one you thought of alone. Be stable, don't freak out and dance the "panic shuffle" as your team stands by watching and waiting for direction, they want the problems to be behind them just as bad as you but without a display of total balance they may doubt your scattered reconciliation. Once you know what a problem's sure fix may be, quickly and clearly delegate the next steps to get your team through the valley and to the mountaintop. When the problem is conquered, modestly celebrate the success with your team and genuinely thank them for their work, input, or patience during your unusual event. This will give them a sense of inclusion and appreciation that will encourage them in the future to be eagerly supportive in helping you find the value of your next "X" factor.

Proverbs 11:14

"Where there is no wise guidance, the nation falls, but in the multitude of counselors there is victory"

    Managers, keep in mind you should always analyze the ways you handle and fix the problems that surface in your restaurant once the dust settles. Being able to develop your analysis into a teachable form to educate others for a similar incident in the future that may prevent or quickly resolve it, is one of the best choices you can make. This will help owners and their managers and possibly all staff, groom their problem solving skills needed for their roles. If you are newer to the management world don't feel discouraged or less than, if you don't think the fastest on your feet just yet, just know your time is coming sooner than not because you see, these types of skills aren't on sale in some department store, neither can they be ordered and express shipped through companies like Amazon Prime. Oh no, these skills have to simply, wisely and deliberately be developed. With the use of your five senses, common sense, dedication, self discipline, and a positive attitude you will be able to develop this superpower called problem solving that all managers and leaders must have during daily operations.

> "You may not be able to control every situation and its outcome, but you can control your attitude and how you deal with it."
>
> -Anonymous

Do you have an emergency action plan for your business? Is it in an area that your staff is aware of and up to date? If not who can prepare one for you?

_____

_____

_____

_____

If a natural disaster strikes are you prepared to delegate and execute a plan to protect your people products and important records? Is your management team mentally prepared or have at least browsed this plan? If you do not have plans in place give yourself a deadline to create it and follow through.

_____

_____

_____

_____

When an emergency strikes would you say your own demeanor is calm and confident? Which manager on your team has challenges with being positive in an unusual situation? In what ways can they work on their reactions? Which manager on your team is great at reacting? Name a time when they displayed this strength.

_____
_____

_____
_____

SECTION 8

CHANGE IS GOOD, NOT!

"Lack of consistency can bring on a lack of interest"

-Unknown

SURPRISE! We are currently out of our world famous fries so we have some crinkle cut potatoes we purchased from the local Wal-Mart for you to enjoy instead and we are also subbing out our black eye peas for snap peas in our signature side. Just a heads up, the burger you love to order that we always season just right is now going to come unseasoned since our cook says it takes too long for him to properly season it the way we used to. We also no longer greet the table with fresh, complementary basket of bread; you must request it and we now charge per roll. Also, instead of being waited on by an employee that is cheerful, having more than enough time to accurately guide you through the menu and inform you of today's specials, we have assigned your table to Wendy who is one of only 3 servers on this busy Friday night and barely has the time to take your drink order let alone remember to bring it to your table. We hope you like the changes we have made and please look forward to even more changes next week as well, because at this time we are in a rollercoaster transition.

Although this is fictional in a sense of menu items and named characters, the scenarios are pretty accurate for a lot of restaurants throughout our nation. That's right, if this is happening under the roof of your business, you are not alone. An unfortunate epidemic that can demolish your flow of clientele is happening all over the country and it's called, inconsistency. One main ingredient that all restaurants must establish and execute well is consistency within their brand; this establishes the reputations connected to your concept. The last thing most people want when they return to a restaurant or familiar brand is to be surprised; as a society we actually like predictability. Your team should have the ability to replicate recipes and continue to produce a customer's favorite dish time and time again along with producing a great guest experience very visit no matter which employee's section they land in for the day.

    There was a new sandwich shop that opened in my hometown that intrigued many people our city and was flooded with new business after being publicized in the local paper. After monitoring their reviews and fining a few that were not so great, I decided I would stop by to inspect their operations further I made a ton of notes from a consumer's perspective that I was able to share with the owner. Most reviews read that the sandwiches were really good, while many reviews expressed long waits and lack of product or ingredients and when I talked to staff separately about the build of their most popular sandwich they all started their sentence with "Well the way that I make it is……" Of course in my mind I was thinking "wait a minute, what do you mean the way that YOU make it?" I was sure at this point that the same sandwich was being prepared differently every day, on every shift; every time and the guests were being made aware of this inconsistency. The amount of meat, the number of cheese slices and volume of toppings were a guessing game at this point so of course, it was time to take out the recipe book and get these employees on track. I was determined to guide the staff toward producing a quality product the way the brand wants it to be, each time no matter who is working or who handles that particular sandwich. After my request for the recipe book, the owner quickly responded "We don't have that; they already know how to make them, every person back there already knows how to make all our sandwiches." This was not the right response for more reasons than one because the truth was they didn't. A manager or owner must lead the charge with consistently following proper recipes and procedures, this goes for any restaurant on the planet. I had to explain the importance of consistency of product and why it was vital for his business to have these tools to benefit the knowledge of the staff, proper inventory, and ultimately financial profit.

    Consistency is the application of something, typically that which is necessary for the sake of logic, accuracy, or fairness. The word I would like to focus on within this definition is "fairness". Most guests would agree that it is completely unfair to fall in love with a signature menu item that your business offers accompanied by great service and as a result they go out and tell their friends and family. This guest shares their experience as a walking billboard for your restaurant and the next week they return with a couple of friends ready to order the same item possibly salivating at the mere thought ready to enjoy the experience they heard so much about. Once the food is placed in front of the guest and they can already see the appearance in presentation is different, and a slight fog of disappointment hovers over them as their thoughts wonder if it will now have the same flavor. To their surprise the flavor profile, unfortunately, is completely different and they just ordered the same item only a week ago. How could this be? So somewhere in production, the 'logic' and 'accuracy' parts in the above definition for consistency seem to have gotten lost in the sauce. This simple disconnect is a catalyst for an unhappy guest, remember unhappy guests don't always complain to upper management they just simply, never return. Now that walking billboard that brought you new patrons, is flashing neon, warning others to keep out. So how do we create and manage consistency is our restaurants?

Psalm 106:3

"Blessed are they who maintain justice; who constantly do what is right."

Owners and managers should create specific and realistic goals when it comes to their particular concept, because it's hard to be consistent if you don't have a strong idea of what you need to do. It's hard to delegate and lead when you don't know where you're going while staying consistent for your team. Yes, we all understand the team members can become bored doing routine work which gives them the moral fuel to fudge or cut corners when it comes to preparation. It is the responsibility of the assigned leaders to manage and maintain proper procedures are followed and continuously hold staff accountable. Create a step by step plan for your concept and set standards that are clear and forward from day one and be sure to communicate them to each employee that will be involved in the process. Once communicated, these standards should be a part of the employee's training as they learn to operate in their hired role. Training sets your staff up for success when you provide them the accurate and up to date tools they need to do their job well. It happens too often that an employee is hired and someone has to explain to them that some of the questions on a menu test may look weird since you no longer carry those particular items. This is an example of how businesses do not provide employees with the right tools to succeed because that can mean items you actually carry are missing as well.

*** Side Note: Please keep in mind that training never stops, new hires go through a training process, only to find out that the skills they were told to display were not being practiced by coworkers or upheld by management and this is a recipe for foundation failure. So, always train, always test keep your staff up to date and on their toes.

Ways to help with consistency in menu items is to keep portion sizes under control. This is also play a huge role with keeping your food cost in line as well. Managers need to be sure cooks and chefs are double checking that each meal is served in proper portions, this can be streamlined by measuring out ingredients like meats, cheeses, or sauces so no matter who is in the kitchen the portion sizes will be standardized. A kitchen manual or recipe book needs to be created with details to help staff during training and production to reference. Be sure this manual is clear, updated, and readily available without having to have a team search to locate it, in a high volume time of need. A great idea would be to have two separate recipe books, one for prep purposes and the second filled with cooking directions and plate presentation to be kept on the cook's line at all times. This is something that proved to be very helpful to my team in operations and also during training. Try to not have a book that is hand written in pen, pencil, or marker, so that staff can quickly read without guessing what alphabets have been scribbled after an item's given measurement. This is a must have for your business to operate smoothly.

Owners, sticking to one main concept and doing it well is a key to restaurant success. Sometimes when owners sample other cuisines they can tend to lose focus on their original food concepts and possibly lose regular clientele also. If you are the hardcore adventurous type, always remember to do your research on new trends and master a way to apply them without losing sight of the core concept, but keep in mind not every trend will work for every business. Managers must stand on the foundation of knowing that at the end of the day your guest's only desire is quality food and service every time they enter your doors. Your patrons should be able to trust you and your teams to deliver the best product so no matter what, train your servers and cooks that before products leave the kitchen it must be right and once that type of culture is established, consistency will become second nature.

> **"Trust is maintained when values and beliefs are actively managed. If companies do not actively work to keep clarity, discipline, and consistency in balance, then trust starts to break down"**
>
> **-Simon Sinek**

Which area of your restaurant seems to embody consistent operation the best Front of House or Back of House? Why do you feel the other area is lacking?

_____
_____

_____
_____

Does your kitchen use a recipe book? Is it updated? Is it in good shape? Which employees misuse this resource? List them. Delegate a manager on your team will get these cooks on track with following proper procedure.

_____
_____

_____
_____

How do you handle a situation with an angry guest who confronts a server about the consistency of your food? In what way could this be avoided? In what way could you fix the situation and retain their business?

_____
_____

_____
_____

Which manager on your team has a challenge with holding employees accountable in the realm of consistency? What are two tips the manager who is great at this task can give? If no managers on your team are holding staff accountable come up with an immediate action plan.

_____
_____

_____
_____

SECTION 9

"38 HOT"

"Mistakes and pressure are inevitable; the secret to getting past them is to stay calm"

-Travis Bradberry

"WHERE IS THE MANAGER?" I WANT TO SEE A MANAGER RIGHT NOW!" The moment an operator or supervisor hears this exclamation; there is an emotional grip that travels to some area in your body, as you brace for the next series of events. This feeling was one of my least favorite to have as a manager. When the demanding anger in a customer's voice quickly reaches your ears, you may want to run and hide; despite the assertive response you agreed to give in these situations during orientation. We have all seen the viral, angry customer compilation videos of customers in a full on shouting match with on duty managers and even hourly staff. Customers that turn napkin holders and receipt printers into flying missiles, towards the cook line or cashier stands as they display their adult sized tantrums. While all of the unwanted excitement is going in these restaurants, they also have the unofficial action journalist filming the breaking news with their android or smart phone going live on social media. These uncomfortable and operationally hindering moments are seen by millions of viewers whether consumers come across it in their very own social media feeds or a coworker gives you that "you have to see this" face and plays the violent reel at your desk. People that can reach this height of anger triggered by a particular circumstance have been referred to as being "38 Hot".

Proverbs 14:17

"A quick tempered person does foolish things, and the one who devises evil schemes is hated."

The definition of "38 Hot", which originated in the south, can be found in the urban dictionary and refers to someone being pissed off to the point of pulling out a gun. Extremely mad, pissed, steamed, aggravated, annoyed is given as the secondary definition. This is the exact persona of the customers in some of those viral videos I just mentioned. The viral videos of the lady that was furious about the ice cream machine being down at a McDonalds and even the screeching, screaming lady that left a Starbucks after hanging up a phone call but not before she ruined the entire, relaxed vibe of that venue which ended with the employees locking the door in fear. These moments are hard to train or prepare for because of their genuine timing and variance of danger. Also living in a country where mental illness and intoxication is also a huge factor, the discernment of using general customer service standards and procedures is hard to figure out, but are pretty much out of the window depending on the severity of the situation. After all the word "anger" is just one letter short of "danger". As owners and managers you have a responsibility to keep your staff safe no matter what, but you must also take into consideration the protection and safety of your patrons that are visiting your establishment. So needless to say the way you handle an extremely angry and possibly dangerous customer must be with urgency and with everyone's best interest in mind. This is very challenging but this is also an opportunity for an owner or manager to exercise their problem solving skills.

Proverbs 15:1

"A gentle answer turns away wrath, but a harsh word stirs up anger"

Now let's look at the number 38 from a different perspective. "In essence the numerology number 38 is about relationships; creative relationships, it also has an inherent talent for dealing with people in a creative and sensitive way. Relationships, teamwork, companionship, coexistence, charisma, intuition, diplomacy, tolerance these are all aspects of the number 38." Complete opposite end of the reactive or personality scale, as it refers to a person being "38 Hot", right? Those are the types of guests we don't mind dealing with, or at least it makes work life much easier to handle. Now let's discuss the ways that we can turn a guest that is displaying a "38 Hot" reaction in your business to a guest that will exude a Numerological "38" reaction.

First, managers must remember to remain calm because there will be absolutely no gain in getting on a customer's level that is yelling or cursing in your business. Because we are only human this may be a true challenge for a lot of leaders especially depending on your personality make up, but you must remember not to take these tantrums personal but focus on the root of the problem and work on producing a dissolving solution. Remember the customer isn't necessarily mad at you as an individual but angry about the product or service not being right or what was expected, and that can be in the aspect of quality, quantity or the interaction that you provided. If the guest has not become violent, a threat to staff or other patrons, be sure to listen and empathize with them dealing with their complaint. The average angry guest just needs to simply vent. The way venting works in any environment requires a person to be the listening ears; managers, you are those listening ears. Don't be a listening ear whose posture or body language is screaming "I could care less" or "Are you really complaining about this? There are starving kids in Africa" a customer's radar will pick this up, very quickly adding fuel to the fire. By you listening carefully you can usually diffuse the situation as long as the customer feels acknowledged. You can solidify you acknowledgment for them by repeating a summary of what you heard and ask questions to have clarity of the complaint.

Proverbs 9:11

"A person's wisdom yields patience; it is to ones glory to overlook an offense"

Respect and understanding go a long way, so expressing sympathy is very important when trying to settle down an irate guest in your establishment. They want to know that you as the manager, truly understands where they are coming from and why they a feeling the way that they feel. What if their compliant is not legit? Well, that's when you make the decision of wanting to keep them as a customer or not, but if you would like to keep them coming around giving you sales it does not matter the validity of their complaint because their perception is now your reality. A simple, but genuine apology is what is required "I'm sorry you're not happy with your our service let's see what we can do to make it right" then it's time to find a solution and follow through on any arrangements or promises.

Colossians 3:12

"Clothe yourselves with compassion, kindness, humility, gentleness, and patience."

So Let's take a reality break; In my career I have had guests that just know there is a guarantee of a discount, comp, or gift anytime that they voice a complaint due to company policy or standard that's actually put in place for the real mistakes, growing pains, or errors during operation. This type of guest you will never be able to please, they make sure of it. This is the way they know they will not pay full price for products of service received. It's very wrong and very annoying to be honest and can really put a squeeze on profitability in the long run. I want to tell you how to handle this type of patron. First, if you recognize them from visiting often to run this scheme, only the managers should deal with this person to further insure that everything is the way they ask and order. Then, repeat, repeat, repeat, and confirm, confirm, confirm and then repeat again point to pictures if you have them available; as crazy as it seems they will find a loop hole to squirm through if you do not. Then go into the kitchen and prepare the food or only have your highest ranked most trusted cook to prepare the food and follow up with a quality check with the guest BEFORE the leave your property. Look them in the eyes professionally and politely and confirm everything is how they want it to be and then send them along the way with a "thanks for coming in, come back and see us soon" you should feel secure and covered. If there is a patron you deal with that does this unfair routine of complaining too often go with your gut and politely tell them "we seem to be unable to make you happy on any of your visits even when the quality of the product is well within our brand standards so we unfortunately will not be able to accommodate you any further since we can't seem to get it right for you, we apologize". Do not let these people use the dusty old saying "the customer is always right" to steal from you in any way. Managers, while you are taking this all in please remember to always use your better judgment and choose your battles wisely when making these types of decisions. You must be sure to keep a log on your desktop or maybe even a clipboard in your office, which your team can access for any replacements with customer names for any Togo orders especially of guests that had a refund processed or credit awarded. You can even set your policy guidelines that require a copy of a receipt or return of the improper food. Once again, be very wise with these decisions, while handling complaints on case by case bases.

    Managers it's very important to call for backup with in-house security or your city police department if a guest is violent or cannot seem to be calmed down. Do not wait long so that they have more time to act out and possibly escalate a situation that could suggest harming themselves or others. Pick up the phone or ask an employee to quickly dial 911 and be calm, realistic and informative so they can come out and extract that particular guest from the property. I highly recommend calling only when actually needed not for minor things because the urgency of the uniformed response may become slowed with the mindset that you cry wolf too often. Once again, this will be an event where you will have to use your better judgment and make the best decision for everyone around you. I also recommend that if you have to call the law, that particular patron should be trespassed so they do not repeat this tantrum in your establishment again and you can keep you workers and visitors safe. Leaders, after the resolution of an angry guest that has taken you completely away from general operations take a minute to regroup so that you can be efficient for the rest of your shift. Dealing with guest complaints can be very stressful and mentally draining, especially if they become "38 Hot", no one wants to be at gunpoint or in a physical altercation over chicken nuggets or milkshakes. So shake it off and find someone on your team that may make you laugh, take a few deep breaths and move on with your day giving great service and providing great products as you were hired to do.

> "Your most unhappy customers are your greatest source of learning "
>
> -Bill Gates

How do you handle a situation with an angry customer? Why is this the best way when operating in your particular brand?

_____
_____

_____
_____

How would you handle an angry guest complaining over the phone, that does not have a receipt?

_____
_____

_____
_____

Do you have a signal or maybe a safe word that means to dial 911 in case a customer becomes violent in your facility? If not create one now and write it below.

_____
_____

_____
_____

How do you calm down after dealing with an extremely angry guest? In what ways do you keep your staff calm when guests decide to quickly approach them in a negative way?

_____
_____

_____
_____

SECTION 10

" BURNOUT BATTLEGROUND"

"No matter what comes your way, shake it off and move forward. When you have a positive mindset, you can't be defeated."

-Joel Osteen

As I heard the brakes of the yellow school bus outside my window I flung my head off of my pillow peeked out the window and yelled "Awe man for real?" while stepping one foot after the other out of the bed and onto the floor. My daughter had just missed the bus again for the fourth Monday in a row. The good news is there was still a chance for her to get to school on time if we hurried, since we lived close by. I went into her room to get her up, trying not to make her panic, because as young as she was, she was the most responsible kid I knew and she hated being late. After flying through the bathrooms and closets of our home and getting her presentable enough to go out into the world we hopped in the car and made a beeline toward her elementary school. When I pulled into the parking lot, I was too late. The car rider line was gone and the school bell had rung, looking up I saw the disappointment on her face in the rearview mirror and I felt like the size of an ant. We walked in the front office and it was then that I realized that I didn't prepare myself to be presentable in public along with my daughter. My hair was crazy, my eyes had huge bags and were still tinted red, I had crust in the crease of my eyes, my clothing didn't match, and my voice was raspy from yelling at work all night. The way the clerk looked at me I could read her mind and envision her thoughts of me as a neglectful parent that struggled with a huge drug problem. I was truly embarrassed. The truth is I got off work around 3:30 a.m. that morning and after my half hour drive to pick up my daughter I then drove us home, laid down to sleep around 4:15 a.m. and 6:05 is when the bus arrived to our house. Not much time for beauty sleep, which explains why I appeared to be Quasimodo was standing in the elementary school's front office. In a matter of hours the bus would bring my daughter back home and I would immediately head to the babysitter's and then head to work to do it all over again.

Romans 12:12

"Be joyful in hope, patient in affliction, and faithful in prayer"

I loved being a manager, even with the extremely long hours; I wanted to be the go to person for any issues, complaints or to pump up the team before a shift. I wanted to have a hand in everything while assuring my staff and guests that I wouldn't let them down. I loved the buzz of my restaurant and I loved the fact that no one day was like another. Like my old area supervisor Brian Smith says "you can't get this working at a bank" he always reminded me even though it gets hard in this industry it is nothing else like it, and I agree. But was I taking on too much? Was I spreading myself too thin trying to be the problem solver and motivator for every moment or issue that arose during my shifts? My staff depended on me for quite a bit and I never refused a question or turned down the opportunity to listen to a new idea. I also trained my staff that If they called or text me I would always answer or respond even on my days off. One day my reality finally clicked, I was married to my job. Physically I had off days on the schedule but work always, successfully leaked into my day all the time through some form of communication. Although I loved being able to help this really began to weigh on my marriage, it began to distract me from family time, and helped me to slowly develop anxiety and depression.

Isaiah 41:10

"Fear not, for I am with you; be not dismayed, for I am your God; I will strengthen you, I will help you, I will uphold you with my righteous right hand."

A position in management is not easy whatsoever, wearing many hats and juggling many demands from all angles that weigh on your ability to rest, relax, and have quality of life at the right times can cause stress, which can cause burnout. Occupational burnout is real and can be a hindrance to both your work and home lifestyles. You may already be experiencing some burnout if you feel that every day at work is a bad day, feel exhausted most of the time, feel no joy or interest in your work, feel overwhelmed by your responsibilities, or have less patience with others than you used to. If you do not get help with the emotional side of what you're feeling, you can also experience physical symptoms such as chest pain, shortness of breath, sleeplessness or heart palpitations so, I want to share a few tips on how to gear up and conquer on the burnout battleground.

Psalm 119:27

"Cause me to understand the way of your precepts that I may meditate on your wonderful deeds."

*****Recognize** the causes of your stress. So, a lot of times when we are in a situation we ask ourselves "how did I get here" and this is a great question, because it's the first step in establishing the desire to find a solution. You may recognize some of the culprits of your stress to be your employees, overwhelming you with too many questions or ideas at all the wrong times. Set a timeframe on which they can bring their comments to you if it's not an emergency, possibly looking into an email avenue only, with allotted time for responses that work well for you and your schedule. Also, don't jump toward every raised hand for every little thing during operation, every single time; this will force staff to figure out some things for themselves which in return may empower them as employees when they are on the job instead of being codependent to the management team.

*****Remember** why you took the job in the first place. Even if your reason was simply because of money to survive, remind yourself of how grateful you are to have the job in the first place. Change your mindset from "I have to do this" over to "I get to do this" and It will help in some of those stressful moments. We all tell our entire family and post on social media about our excitement of getting hired or promoted but we lose that glow after some time for many reasons, but try to reminisce on some of those beginning days, to help you sift out any discouragement. Also keep in mind, that someone saw something in you to allow you the opportunity to become a manager and lead a group of people while helping to run a business and that speaks volumes about how the people in your company see you as an individual. That's a great reason to shake the stress and continue moving up.

*****Reevaluate** your personal life and activities outside of work. Are you spending time with your family or spouse making new memories? Are you eating the right foods and getting enough sleep? These are very important questions to ask yourself to adjust your habits and ensure that you have a good work life balance. Having the discipline to turn off your phone or not responding to any work emails is the way to go. If you're a manager that's not doing this just yet, now is the time for you to begin.

*****Relax** as often as you can because this is the breeding ground for severe burnout if not taken seriously. To relax is not the same as getting sleep. You may relax by writing which is a great tool, because it forces you to be still and take time to yourself to express your thoughts or ideas. You may relax by meditation, reading, massage, or even lounging on the beach. Music is also a great way to relax by listening to your favorite songs completely tuning out the rest of the world and taking that time for yourself. These are all great ways to accomplish a relaxed state, just don't forget that the most important part is to DO IT!

Although managing a restaurant is a very challenging job, it can be very rewarding as well if done properly. The few tips listed above are only some that I chose to highlight that are available out there, but the goal is to find exactly what can work for you, as an individual, while keeping in mind that this is no overnight fix or remedy for burnout, but will take time along with dedication. When you use these tips to conquer stress you have a better chance at producing a better version of yourself when it's time to perform at work. Reduction or elimination of burnout will allow you to think clearly and execute tasks more efficiently during you shifts making you a better leader for your team to follow and someone the company can truly depend on.

> "For fast-acting relief, try slowing down"
>
> – Lily Tomlin

What two changes will you make first to relieve the stress in your life?

_____
_____

_____
_____

Would you consider keeping a journal as a way to combat anxiety? If you already have a journal how often do you use it?

_____
_____

_____
_____

Do you have someone that you could talk to in a time of strong depression or anxiety? If yes who is that person? If not who could you designated someone for that role?

_____
_____

_____
_____

Does your company award vacation time? Do you actually take it? If yes, what are your plans for you next one? If you are not taking them, why? When will you begin?

_____
_____

_____
_____

Thank You

I appreciate you so much for taking the time out to read my book allowing me to share my stories and experience with you. Thank you for reading my tips on how to prevent your restaurant's culture from going up in flames, for some owners and manager's you may view this book containing the tips to help you put out the flames destroying your culture at this time. Regardless, if you take away just one great thing that you can go into your store and implement to enhance the culture and make your life in operations easier, it's equal to a hundred wins for me. Please remember your challenges are not exclusive and we must all show love, compassion, and help one another. Good luck to you and your team in this amazing, challenging, and rewarding industry and always remember to keep God first in your life.

"Do not despise these small beginnings, for the Lord rejoices to see the work begin..."

Zachariah 4:10

MY RESTAURANT IS ON FIRE

NOTES

MY RESTAURANT IS ON FIRE

MY RESTAURANT IS ON FIRE

MY RESTAURANT IS ON FIRE

MY RESTAURANT IS ON FIRE

MY RESTAURANT IS ON FIRE

www.ingramcontent.com/pod-product-compliance
Lightning Source LLC
Chambersburg PA
CBHW051325220526
45468CB00004B/1500